EDUCATED SMOKER

DSFPlan

MICHAEL OLIVER

Order this book online at www.trafford.com
or email orders@trafford.com

Most Trafford titles are also available at major online book retailers.

© Copyright 2014 Michael Oliver.

Printed in the United States of America.

ISBN: 978-1-4907-2230-6 (sc)
ISBN: 978-1-4907-2232-0 (hc)
ISBN: 978-1-4907-2231-3 (e)

Library of Congress Control Number: 2013923680

The views expressed in this work are solely those of the author and do not necessarily reflect
the views of the publisher, and the publisher hereby disclaims any responsibility for them.

Any people depicted in stock imagery provided by Thinkstock are models,
and such images are being used for illustrative purposes only.
Certain stock imagery © Thinkstock.

Trafford rev. 02/27/2014

 www.trafford.com

North America & international
toll-free: 1 888 232 4444 (USA & Canada)
fax: 812 355 4082

CONTENTS

Educated Smoker
Gifts To You
DSF Plan To Assist

WRITE YOUR FULL NAME HERE

To Help You To Teach
Yourself How To Stop
Smoking Forever

Demolish Smoking
Forever Plan Is A
Personal Study Guide

That Will
Indeed Help
You Too

STATEMENT OF LIABILITY WAIVER:

Simply having suspicions alone about tobacco smoking, leads me to believe that, every person smoking cigarettes or chewing tobacco should know, it is their duty to know exactly what they are doing and why they are doing it, along with what hazards they may or may not be involved with, during the actions being taken, while smoking cigarettes and using tobacco in other ways. Therefore, between the covers of this book, is a helpful stop smoking personal study guide, that did help me and should very well help each individual, in their own attempt to stop smoking in a satisfying way. It is not being claimed that this book will help anyone, who doesn't wish to put the little effort needed into quitting, but to help those who do perform to put the little effort needed to quit smoking. For the previous reasoning here within, this book will be published with the user's understanding only, that all liability hazards and risk supposedly caused by this user's guide, be waived at the expense of the complaining readers using this material. Reader's of this guide will use and read at their own risk and excuse any errors created by the Author. Possession of this book is your acceptance to these rules. Ignorance is no excuse to the rules.

Mom & Dad   Diana, Denise, Michael & Darla

Michael, Mom & Dad   Imelda & Michael

Vincent & John   Mom, Michael & Imelda

ABOUT THE AUTHOR

Hi, I am Michael Oliver. Allow me to share briefly about my life with you. I am the third child and only son of Claudia Hunt W. and Richard Calvin Oliver. I was born in Redding, California, USA. It was Friday, 11:12 PM on March 21, 1958. A cold wet evening, 49° and had rained a little over one half inch for the day.

Anderson, a city south of Redding is where I lived for nineteen months. Before I was two years old, my dad was laid off from U. S. Plywood. He found a new mill job with G. P. Corporation in Samoa, California. Our family home was in Eureka just across Humboldt Bay from Samoa, where my three sisters and I were raised. Their names are, Diana Kay, Cassie Denise and Darla Jeanne. **ref.** Our dad past on May 24, 1997 at age 67. Mom is living in Chico, California and just turned 75 March 9, 2013.

At the age of twelve I started playing with cigarettes. Not fulltime, but as often as I could pocket one to smoke. This brings back memories, trying to find cigarettes to smoke. I felt like a total bum at times and did a lot of smoking where someone else left off.

Looking back into my high school days at St. Bernard's High School, back then, my classmates knew me as "Smoke," the nickname they gave me. This had me feeling proud to smoke.

After graduating in June of 1976, I spent time working making a dollar or two. It seemed as though I learned many different jobs as a teenager growing up. Welding Crab Pots was one of the choices I had and I enjoyed doing it. But living in Eureka or should I say the "Fog" was too cold for me. I needed to go and look around for some sunshine. I took a trip with my boss, Burt Tirey, to the Sacramento Valley area to visit his mother, Ruth Goodman. A few months later in May of '78, Burt, Bill and I moved to Grimes, California. Fog was known as seasonal only here in this valley. **ref.** Burt past on February 25, 2003 at age 62.

My work history in '78 started out as a night janitor at Eskaton Hospital in Colusa, California. Three months later I found myself working at a truck stop in Dunnigan, California. One week into that, the "EDD" sent me to a new job back in Colusa. I took on their job working with FMC Corporation, processing vine seed.

Thinking back to my earlier life, I started out working at the age of nine as a gardener. I found working to be fun since I was making 10 cents per hour cutting grass. Planting vegetables at some of those locations turned out to be another job I enjoyed. Helping dad in his garden and since he was raised on a farm, it helped me to up-grade my knowledge in gardening. It always seemed to amaze me though, how these little seeds could grow such wonderful fruit in life. By the time I was eighteen, I was still gardening, hauling bee hives all over Humboldt County, along with working at a gas station and building crab pots on the side. I really enjoyed working at my younger age and wished it were possible to continue on those terms, you know, keeping your entire check. Now and since then I live in the real world now, paying my taxes which are withheld from my check.

The following is a list of the companies I've worked for over the years in their order. Eureka Cash Oil, Burt's Custom Pot, Eskaton Hospital, Dunnigan Truck Stop, FMC Corporation, S&K Railroad Company, Thayer Aviation, Niagara Seeds, Celanese Corporation, Moran Seeds, Tarke Warehouse, Weslam Food Warehouse, Ziegenmeyer Farms, Parris Valley Campers, Tokano Farms, Fedora Farms, Harris Moran Seeds and Bonanza Seeds International, Inc.

I got married for the first time October 19, 1989 and divorced (Not by choice) January 8, 1999 after raising two boys. Their names are, C. Vincent Lawson III and John Lewis Lawson.

John became a U. S. Marine after graduating from Colusa High School in June of 1998. I can remember John's graduation from Boot Camp, how proud his mother and I were to have a son who was making the right choices in life. John served two consecutive terms in the Marine Core before thinking he'd look for work on the outside. John had great plans to become a State/Gov. employee until they found out he was color blind, they wouldn't let him into his field. John being a little sad from that decided the best move for him now would be to enlist into the U. S. Army, to retire from the service in about nine more years or so. The weekend before John had to leave into the Army, Luisa and John came to my side business to let me know I was going to be a grandpa and that they were planning to get married in a couple hours or so before John has to leave.

Vincent on the other hand decided to become a U. S. Marine after John graduated from Boot Camp. I'm sure Vincent had notice just as his mother and I did, how neatly and sharp John looked as a U. S. Marine and Vincent wanted that too. I will never forget when Vincent told me about the time they got off the bus at Boot Camp. He was standing there in line up with an itch on his nose and decided he'd scratch it. How that drill instructor got in his face and told Vincent that he is no longer in charge of himself anymore. I really wondered if that's all it took, because I tried for years with love and never seemed to work that easy for me. Vincent has completed his one term in the Marine Core and has moved on to another life on the outside. Shannon and Vincent have three boys now, just after having twins, March 30, 2010. Vincent is in the grocery business, living in Rockford, Michigan.

I have married for the second time with Imelda Bozar in Manlilipot, Albay, Philippines on October 17, 2002. We first met in Singapore where Imelda was working. Imelda has six brothers, three sisters and two are here in the USA, Carmen and Veronica. Agrepina is living in the Philippines along with her four brothers', Antonio, Sancho, Noe, and Pedro. Two brothers' have past away, Cornello and Romeo. We lost Imelda's mother, Luisa on February 20, 2004. Imelda lost her dad, Francisco when she was nineteen.

It's kind of funny how Imelda and I met. Dan, Carmen and I were all on the same bowling league team in the summer of 2000. Carmen wanted to share a picture of her sister "Imelda" with me. Of course that was just the beginning. Carmen asked, "Do you like the picture?" Yes, she looks nice, of course that's what I said. When I gave the picture back, Carmen said, "No you can keep it, I have others." So, I put the picture in my pocket without a struggle.

After several weeks at league bowling, Carmen asked if I had heard from Imelda? "No, I haven't heard." Carmen's next step is getting her sister to call me. Then finally one day it happens, I receive a message on my answering machine, Imelda from Singapore called about 2 PM while I was at work. The following bowling evening Carmen asks, "Did you here from Imelda?" "Yes." "Oh, did you call her back?" No, not yet. Carmen said, "Mike, I have a $5.00 phone card I want to give you. This is the least expensive way to call Imelda." Let me tell you folks now, Carmen was right, that card really got me going. Ended up calling Imelda on daily bases. Woke her in the morning before her work and put her to bed at night from the distant miles away.

December 12, 2003 I welcomed Imelda into the USA at the San Francisco International Airport. This was truly a very special and happy day for us in our lives. Finally, together for keeps. The drive home took about two hours to Live Oak, California. We are on our way for a new beginning. On our drive home Imelda asked, "How come they leave all the dead trees standing?" Of course it was my pleasure to let Imelda know that the trees aren't dead, they're dormant this time of the year in our area.

Since her arrival, Imelda has had to adjust to the cold and foggy weather of winter. Philippines weather is quite different than we have here. They are tropical and when it rains, it flat out pours, but the weather stays warm. The Philippine sea shores look like the shores at Lake Tahoe, Nevada. California ocean shores remind Imelda of the typhoon weather over in the Philippines.

Imelda and I have traveled by car to many more places than I can mention here, but I will point out a few. From San Francisco shores up the California, Oregon Coast to Belington, Washington. Live Oak, California to Yakima, Washington, down through Idaho and back up to and across Wyoming to Keystone, South Dakota. One other trip we took to Yakima, we drove up to Okanagan Lake to Kelowna, Canada. What a story book drive this turned out to be and with the most beautiful sites that Canada has to offer.

In March of 2009, Imelda and I flew to Manila, Philippines. From there we met up with my business associates to look over some of their production sites for the next few days in the Laoag, Philippines area. From there, back to Manila and on to our final destination to Tiwi, Albay, Philippines, Imelda's home where she was raised. The hand labor here truly amazes me how hard these rice farmers work to get a sack of rice. If they only knew of our way here in USA, it would make their job so much more efficient.

In July 2010, we drove over the country back roads from Sacramento, California to Las Vegas, Nevada. On a tour, Imelda and I flew front seat helicopter over the Hoover Dam, to the West Rim of the Grand Canyon and back over the Las Vegas City Strip.

One month later, we took our first trip to Waikiki, Hawaii. We stayed at Maile Sky Court which gave us a beautiful view of the city and ocean sites. Imelda's sister Veronica and brother in-law Ted made sure our stay was very pleasant during the evening times. In the day time hours, we visited sites by foot and tour bus.

INTRODUCTION TO DSF PLAN

DSF Plan was first introduced to the public in July of 1994. Since then, has been distributed through mail order to those in need of a satisfying way to stop smoking. Congratulations and welcome on your decision to gain knowledge of what is the safest and surest way ever in helping users to stop smoking as painlessly and as easily as possible. DSF Plan has a unique approach that allows its users, to quit without even really realizing, how they did stop smoking. Users are saying, "It was so easy to quit, how in the world did I do it?" Though, DSF Plan won't do all the work for you, because it does take a little effort from its users, but will help its users in making all their right decisions easier as they read and follow along.

With twenty-three years of experience smoking, I'd have to say, that qualifies me on how I did feel when I attempted not to smoke. When I first started smoking, it came slow. And making it past that little buzz stage which makes most people sick, but once you do, it is that much easier to continue. Of course there had to be some reasons in wanting to start smoking in the first place? My parents both smoked and I wanted to look older than I was, so I figured this would be the way to go. The crazy thing was, at my young age, being caught smoking meant I could get the belt. I couldn't understand why, if it was so safe, what's the big deal? My friend, Bill Carsner had a similar situation. His dad, Frank smoked, but not his mother, Elsie. Seems like Bill's parents knew he smoked and they didn't seem to mind as much as my parents did. Turns out, this was bad because I had a place to go and smoke freely. **ref.** Francis Carsner past on December 29, 1981 at age 57.

The real problem with smoking over the years is hard to handle. It seems as though all I feel like doing is sitting around smoking. I have smoking involved with everything I am doing in my life besides sleeping. I know the best thing for me would be to find a way out, if there is a way to find. I am smoking three and a half packs a day. I can't seem to figure out why I don't feel like I am in control. More like the habit is controlling me. I figure now would be the right time to take action for my life, while I still have the say so in my life.

Being a bit confused about smoking, really became a rude awakening to hear both my parents decided to quit smoking, after loving to smoke for all those years. My dad was able to lay them down cold turkey in March of '84. Mom took a class with her friend, Lauretta Gosvener a few months later and was able to quit, even though Lauretta didn't. **ref.** Lauretta past on July 31, 1998 at age 60.

I have tried to stop smoking before and I know how hard it seems to be. I even tried my Doctor's program once and felt more stress than I could handle. Though, physicians are right most of the time, it would be nice if the non-never smokers could step back out of the way and allow me the needed space I need to conquer this habit with the help of the professionals that I choose. The less head-games I have to deal with from the non-professionals, the easier it will be for me to concentrate on becoming successful. I've learned a lot about smoking, while doing it and trying to quit.

With my life to gain, I have to be honest with you now. Back when I was learning how to quit, it wasn't so easy to tell a friend or anyone else about any issues I may have had and why I needed to quit, because of all the head-games people appear to play. In my case the pain came slowly and worsened the more I smoked. Then the craziest thing happened a few months after I quit smoking. An act of the devil smacked me down in my tracks. I woke up one morning and felt a rough raw pain in my upper left chest area. Seems like this bad smoking pain got worse for some un-Godly reason. I was rushed to the hospital in an ambulance. Turns out after a few test, I had "Pleurisy." Currently, it has been seventeen years ago since I did quit smoking and all my pain gradually disappeared during the first year.

Anyone smoking wanting to quit, have the best stop smoking plan before themselves now and it's forever. DSF Plan is here to help anyone willing to use it. DSF Plan works like gravity and without replacing smoking with some other unwanted routine.

While using DSF Plan, the final improvements were added to this program. It is in my belief now, that DSF Plan is the stop smoking program of the past, present and future. The requirements for using DSF Plan are simple, the users should know how to read, write and follow the simple solutions. If you are willingly able to do that, you will be our next "Educated Smoker."

DSF Plan Instructions

There are six DSF Plan instructional lessons step by step for users to read and follow along. These lessons were wrote in an easy as possible way to demolish smoking forever. Each lesson has an important title, instructional steps and may have an examination section.

Read the instructions before attempting the lesson and follow the lessons step by step to gain control of the lesson to learn. Follow the examination section step by step to bring out into the open what we never seem to consider.

Plan a date ahead before using DSF Plan. Once decided, mark that day on your calendar. When that day arrives, start DSF Plan and use the program from the beginning to the end. Never stop in the middle thinking you have what it will take to stop and stay stopped even if you have stopped smoking. Study all the lessons and do the program all the way through, that will be your added assurance you will need, to demolish smoking forever from your life.

Each lesson may require between twenty-four and seventy-two hours of actually doing the steps in that lesson. Don't take it upon yourself to move on to the next lesson, before proving the current lesson's total required hours.

It may take between thirty minutes and up to one hour of studying time for each lesson in one sitting. The best time for studying may be two or three hours before bedtime as a suggestion only. It may be best to sleep with the information you have just received. This will give our mind time to adjust to the different way of thinking. Naturally before sleeping, you will be planning your day ahead the night before. Although, you may have your own study time whenever is right for you. If you are able to read and follow the lessons as you read, this might be best for you.

From lesson two through lesson five, there is a Suggestions and Activities List which will help us to make the best of our extra time we are going to start having. Study the Suggestions/Activities List, because they are here to help us conquer tobacco.

Some of the lessons may require you to have the following materials; Goal Paper which is provided in this book, pen or pencil, a clock or watch with a second hand, an empty container with a lid, a clean ashtray, a brown paper sack and a calculator. The intention of DSF Plan is simple and never should be thought of beyond what the nature of this program was intended for. DSF Plan is simply a personal study guide to help anyone willing and able to use it, to stop smoking in a satisfying way. DSF Plan has no medical background and is not to be mistaken for any medical cure against tobacco smoking. In my own belief, no doctor ever told me to start smoking, so why should it be recognized as a medical problem to quit smoking. If anything, it might be a medical improvement and not a problem.

During and after using DSF Plan, it will be best to continue studying and performing this program along with what you have learned as often as you please. Never tempt yourself into returning to the old routine you wish to put behind you now. Work at your own pace. You are in no race with anyone to see how fast or short of time you can succeed in. If you slip and fall short, stand up with strength and continue to walk forward for best results. You do have what it will take to become successful. Nobody can help _____ more than _____

Mr./Mrs. Your Last Name   Himself/Herself

Each book may come with a .pdf file for PC users for an additional fee. Before planning to study from the "Read, fill in the blanks only" version, you will need to think ahead so the program doesn't get closed before the completion to save your study. To stop a study session you have already started and to save your work for your next session, "Minimize" the program window using the left mouse click at the top right of screen, then left mouse click on "Start" at the bottom left of screen, click on "Turn off computer", click on "Standby". PC is safe until you are ready to go for another session.

Users may "Tab Key" your way to the next blank to fill in during a study session. The paper back study book is needed so your permanent notes can be transferred and kept safe.

After you have completed DSF Plan, "My Very Own Story" on page 47 is for you to write your own reference how DSF Plan worked out for you. Start out by stating your name, how you started, with whom, when, how long you smoked. Be creative.

DSF Plan Lesson One
Awareness

Instructions:

Simply follow the steps in this lesson for twenty-four hours before moving on to Lesson Two. If following the steps become difficult in the exact way they are wrote, it may be best to restart your time over when you last caught yourself doing the steps wrong. Read and fill in the blanks for each step. Study this lesson as often as you please.

Step 1:

It is best never to tell <u>anyone</u> when planning to stop smoking. Keeping it to <u>ourselves</u> that we wish to stop smoking will simply <u>relieve</u> us from many of the <u>pressures</u> of quitting smoking.

It is best never to tell _____ when planning to stop smoking. Keeping it to _____ that we wish to stop smoking will simply _____ us from many of the _____ of quitting smoking.

Step 2:

<u>Remove</u> <u>all</u> cigarettes, matches, lighters and any other tobacco products you may be carrying. After removing them from your <u>pockets</u> or purses, <u>never</u> carry them back in your pockets or purses for the rest of your <u>life</u>.

_____ _____ cigarettes, matches, lighters and any other tobacco products you may be carrying. After removing them from your _____ or purses, _____ carry them back in your pockets or purses for the rest of your _____.

Step 3:

Sometimes, <u>people</u> find themselves reaching or smoking unaware of their <u>knowledge</u> of <u>knowing</u> what they are doing. If you <u>notice</u> this happening to you, <u>stop</u> what you are doing right away. <u>Penalize</u> yourself by <u>not</u> smoking for the next ten minutes.

Sometimes, _____ find themselves reaching or smoking unaware of their _____ of _____ what they are doing. If you _____ this happening to you, _____ what you are doing right away. _____ yourself by _____ smoking for the next ten minutes.

1

Michael Oliver

Step 4:

As long as you <u>plan</u> to continue smoking, it is best to smoke <u>King</u> <u>Filter</u> <u>Lights</u> or a lighter cigarette. If you smoke anything other than that now, throw away your opened packs and trade in your unopened packs. <u>Never</u> <u>smoke</u> any <u>tobacco</u> without a filter.

As long as you _____ to continue smoking, it is best to smoke _____ _____ _____ or a lighter cigarette. If you smoke anything other than that now, throw away your opened packs and trade in your unopened packs. _____ _____ any _____ without a filter.

Examination 1:

Now it is time to take a look into your smoking routine. Never make the excuse like, "That's not the right figure," because give or take a few thousand either way isn't going to make much difference. Write in the answers to the best of your knowledge. Using a calculator, simply + - × ÷ as instructed.

A. How many packs do you smoke per day? _____
Cigarettes smoked ÷ (20) or (25) cigarettes in a pack = A
B. How much does one pack cost? _____
Cost of a carton ÷ 10 packs in a carton = B
C. How much does it cost to smoke each day? _____
A × B = C
D. How much does it cost to smoke each week? _____
C × 7 = D
E. How much does it cost to smoke each year? _____
D × 52 = E
F. How old are you now? _____
G. How old were you when you first started? _____
H. How many years have you been smoking? _____
F - G = H
I. How much money has been spent smoking? _____
E × H = I

Smoking can add up over the years. Think why you wish to stop.

GOAL PAPER

Michael Oliver

CONGRATULATIONS,

YOU HAVE PASSED

LESSON ONE AND

HAVE COMPLETED

THE LAST TWENTY-

FOUR HOURS

LEARNING

"AWARENESS"

CONTINUE WITH

ALL YOU HAVE

LEARNED AND TAKE

IT WITH YOU TO

LESSON TWO IN

LEARNING

"OUTSIDE FRESHNESS"

DSF Plan Lesson Two
Outside Freshness

Instructions:

Simply follow the steps in this lesson for seventy-two hours before moving on to Lesson Three. If following the steps become difficult in the exact way they are wrote, it may be best to restart your time over when you last caught yourself doing the steps wrong. Read and fill in the blanks for each step. Study this lesson as often as you please.

Examination 2:

You will need the following materials; a clean ashtray, pencil or pen, Goal paper, two cigarettes and a clock/watch with a second hand. On your Goal paper, write the words, "Sitting and burning" and "The one I smoked."

What you are about to do is, to keep track of the time it takes for two cigarettes burning in two different ways. One you will light and let sit in your ashtray burning. You may need to move it around so it doesn't burn out too quickly and let it smoke itself to its butt. Write a starting time down on your Goal paper and then light that cigarette to sit and burn. Write down a starting time for the one you plan to smoke and then light it and smoke as you would any other time. For this test, smoke your cigarette to the butt and keep track of the time it takes. Then write down the time. Never throw away any of your notes, because you may need them in another exercise later.

Step 1:

From now on it may be best <u>not</u> to <u>smoke</u> in your house or <u>anyone's</u> house or any part connected to yours and their house for the rest of <u>your</u> <u>life</u>.

From now on it may be best _____ to _____ in your house or _____ house or any part connected to yours and their house for the rest of _____ _____.

Step 2:

It will be best <u>not</u> to <u>smoke</u> in your car, pickup, truck or anyone's <u>car</u>, pickup or truck for the <u>rest</u> of your life.

It will be best _____ to _____ in your car, pickup, truck or anyone's _____, pickup or truck for the _____ of your life.

Step 3:

<u>Never</u> ever <u>smoke</u> in any closed cab piece of equipment or machinery for the rest of your <u>life</u>. Never ever smoke in any closed room of any <u>kind</u> <u>either</u>.

_____ ever _____ in any closed cab piece of equipment or machinery for the rest of your _____. Never ever smoke in any closed room of any _____ _____.

Note: If you wish to smoke, simply stop what you are doing and go outside for some fresh air.

Step 4:

Never <u>replace</u> smoking cigarettes or the uses of any tobacco with eating or chewing <u>anything</u>. <u>Remember</u>, you are simply trying to loose a <u>habit</u> without gaining anymore new ones. Stick to <u>your</u> <u>diet</u> and drink plenty of <u>water</u>, juices, coffee, tea, milk and any other virgin drink you like.

Never _____ smoking cigarettes or the uses of any tobacco with eating or chewing _____. _____, you are simply trying to loose a _____ without gaining anymore new ones. Stick to _____ _____ and drink plenty of _____, juices, coffee, tea, milk and any other virgin drink you like.

Step 5:

<u>Clean</u> all the areas you no <u>longer</u> <u>wish</u> to smoke in anymore. <u>Try</u> and stay in these areas as much as possible. If you become nervous in any way, <u>simply</u> walk outside to <u>relieve</u> the <u>tension</u>.

_____ all the areas you no _____ _____ to smoke in anymore. _____ and stay in these areas as much as possible. If you become nervous in any way, _____ walk outside to _____ the _____.

DSF Plan Lesson Two
Suggestions/Activities List

Suggestions:

1. All good things take an effort. People are rewarded with the good things of life, with how much effort they are willing to put toward the good things they wish to receive.

2. All people have been created with special qualities about themselves. These special qualities you have give you the excellent ability in helping, yourself to grow out of the old and into the new. You have all the qualities it takes to overcome anything you wish for in your life and more. Our God and Creator knew exactly what to do in creating qualities for

---

Write your full name on the line above

3. You have got what it takes to overcome anything in your life. Think about it, anything you wish to overcome. With the effort you put toward what you wish to overcome, this is your guarantee.

4. You've got the power to overcome by believing in yourself. You have already proved so much this far. Believe in yourself. You can do it. Keep striving forward. Believe in what you can do.

5. Practice using the word "Look" in a different way. Instead of looking for cigarettes to smoke, try not to look for cigarettes to smoke. If you are not looking for cigarettes, you won't be tempted to smoke cigarettes. You know right where they are, but practice passing by them and by not looking at them as you walk by them.

6. When watching TV, plan ahead for breaks. For example, when a commercial comes on, plan to watch it through, take a walk, wet a washcloth and wipe your face, get a drink of water or another cup of coffee or tea. Do other things besides smoking.

7. Let yourself know how good you feel. You are in control of every good thing happening in your life.

8. Don't use the word "Again" at the end of any sentence. Believe it. A person who says, "I'll never do it again," probably is sincere. But, not always able to live by what they may have said. They have left the last said word to remember what they want to forget again.

10

Activities:
1. Taking a simple walk can help the mind to take in new thoughts to think. Sometimes, it is a good idea to start walking and plan as you walk. Other times, planning before you take a walk, where you would like to go is a good idea. Walking up back and forth in your own yard or in a room can even help do some good. Walk in a relaxed position with your head and shoulders dropped can feel good. Of course, watch where you are going.
2. Maybe you would like to catch up on some work you have saved for a rainy day, even if it is not raining. This is a great time to have the time to think. Most jobs are done in routine with only little thinking. This gives us time to think of new thoughts.
3. Riding a bike can help you to take in new thoughts to think. Ask a friend to go riding with you.
4. Visit a friend who doesn't smoke. Watch them closely. Try to figure out how they get along without smoking. It is best not to ask or tell them anything about what you are doing though. They cannot help you with something they have never experienced before. Besides, it is not a good idea to discuss this plan until the right given time. The right time is after you have graduated.
5. Some people like to collect aluminum cans off the streets and highways. This can help us take in new thoughts to think.
6. Other people cannot stand to see trash and litter lying along the streets and highways. Remember to wear bright clothing while walking along roadways.
7. Join a gym in your area or go with a friend to one. With a friend or not, a gym could become a good workout place and a good time for you to take in new thoughts. Some of the nicer gyms have the most updated equipment of today for you to use.
8. Go window-shopping for boats, cars or clothing. This can be another good time to take in new thoughts to think.
9. Plan a trip somewhere you've never been, to find a new site, could be a good time to take in other thoughts to think.

Goal Paper

Michael Oliver

CONGRATULATIONS,

YOU HAVE PASSED

LESSON TWO AND

HAVE COMPLETED

THE LAST SEVENTY-

TWO HOURS

LEARNING

"OUTSIDE FRESHNESS"

CONTINUE WITH

ALL YOU HAVE

LEARNED AND TAKE

IT WITH YOU TO

LESSON THREE IN

LEARNING

"EXTERMINATION"

DSF Plan Lesson Three
Extermination

Instructions:

Simply follow the steps in this lesson for forty-eight hours before moving on to Lesson Four. If following the steps become difficult in the exact way they are wrote, it may be best to restart your time over when you last caught yourself doing the steps wrong. Read and fill in the blanks for each step. Study this lesson as often as you please.

Step 1:

It is best <u>not</u> to buy <u>cigarettes</u> in large quantities for the rest of your <u>life</u>. <u>No</u> <u>more</u> cartons, <u>no</u> <u>more</u> two and three or more packs at a time. <u>Never</u> allow anyone else to buy cigarettes or <u>tobacco</u> products for you either. If you need to buy <u>cigarettes</u>, then buy just <u>one</u> <u>pack</u> each trip to the store.

It is best _____ to buy _____ in large quantities for the rest of your _____. _____ _____ cartons, _____ _____ two and three or more packs at a time. _____ allow anyone else to buy cigarettes or _____ products for you either. If you need to buy _____, then buy just _____ _____ each trip to the store.

Step 2:

Never <u>relight</u> any cigarette that has already been <u>lit</u> whether it <u>burnt</u> out or not. If you wish to <u>smoke</u>, start with a <u>fresh</u> cigarette from your own pack. <u>No</u> <u>more</u> saving it for later. If you run out of <u>cigarettes</u>, don't look for cigarettes and they won't bother you.

Never _____ any cigarette that has already been _____ whether it _____ out or not. If you wish to _____, start with a _____ cigarette from your own pack. _____ _____ saving it for later. If you run out of _____, don't look for cigarettes and they won't bother you.

Step 3:

Don't <u>bum,</u> <u>steal</u> or take <u>cigarettes</u> that are not yours. <u>Never</u> <u>buy</u> cigarettes from a friend at work or anywhere else besides at a store. Never <u>ever</u> <u>take</u> an offer from anyone either. When you have smoked <u>all</u> your cigarettes and you are <u>out,</u> you must do without.

Don't _____, _____ or take _____ that are not yours. _____ _____ cigarettes from a friend at work or anywhere else besides at a store. Never _____ _____ an offer from anyone either. When you have smoked _____ your cigarettes and you are _____, you must do without.

Step 4:
It's best from now on to <u>never</u> ever smoke while standing <u>up</u> for the rest of your <u>life</u>. Don't smoke while working on the <u>job</u> or <u>off</u> the job. It is best to never ever smoke while <u>doing</u> anything. If you wish to smoke, then take the time it takes to smoke, <u>while</u> doing <u>nothing</u> else.

It's best from now on to _____ ever smoke while standing _____ for the rest of your _____. Don't smoke while working on the _____ or _____ the job. It is best to never ever smoke while _____ anything. If you wish to smoke, then take the time it takes to smoke, _____ doing _____ else.

Step 5:
A. You will need a brown paper sack, a clean ashtray, your cigarettes, a lighter, a clock/watch and an empty container with a plastic lid. From now on, carry your cigarettes, matches, ashtray, clock/watch and container in your brown paper sack. If you wear a watch, this is fine.

B. Put some water in the bottom of your empty plastic container just under one quarter full. If you wish to smoke, find a comfortable place to sit, squat or kneel outside. Set your ashtray outside your sack and use it. Limit yourself to one cigarette during one sitting.

C. When you are not puffing on your cigarette, leave it burning in your ashtray. Never share your cigarette with anyone and don't share anyone's cigarette with them either.

D. After you are finished smoking your cigarette, open your container and empty your ashtray out into the water. Put the lid back on tightly and put all your things back into your bag. Clean your container out daily.

E. Never leave your smoking sack unattended. If you are unable to watch your sack, lock it in your car trunk out of reach from children or anyone else.

DSF Plan Lesson Three
Suggestions/Activities List

Suggestions:

1. You are the one in control of every thought that enters your mind. If you don't think the thought, it can't ever bother you. You control every thought you think. Nobody can think a thought for you in your mind. All actions take place when you first think the thought. If your thought is a habit, your brain carries out the action needed to fill the need of the habit. And without you feeling the need to do hardly any thinking about what you are doing. So, now you can understand why it is hard to not do something once it becomes a habit to do. Once you know how to do something, it becomes a habit to do it that certain way. From now on and for the rest of your life, practice what you want to think. If you don't think the thought, the thought can't ever bother you.

2. The urge to smoke is simply triggered by a thought that was thought of while you were thinking. Such as a thought to take a break. Our minds have this thought imbedded into a habit when it is break-time, we automatically think it's smoke time. Only you can control the thought you think. By simply not thinking the thought to smoke, by continuously reminding yourself and planning ahead why you wish to stop smoking in the first place, the urge to smoke will reduce and may never bother you. This will take practice, so practice while you're thinking. A triggered urge can also come from a place where you are standing, sitting or even visiting with a friend or someone else. Be prepared to conquer it.

3. Demolish Smoking Forever. Think while you are thinking to demolish smoking forever. Think to take something and demolish it forever. Think of taking the thought to smoke. To break little pieces off and demolish them is going to be a trick, but it can be done if the pieces are demolished with the proper knowledge. Keep thinking while you think of ways it will take to demolish smoking forever.

Fill in your full name here
does have the knowledge it takes to demolish smoking forever.

19

Activities:
1. Taking a drive through the country can help bring in pleasant thoughts to think.
2. Fishing can be a good pass-time to take up the slack if you're into the sport. It is a wild feeling to have a fish fight on the end of your line.
3. Boating is a way of getting the mind to think new thoughts to think. Being on the water alone gives us the feeling as we're moving double the speed than we really are, 25 mph feels like 50 mph.
4. Hiking can be an experience of letting the mind take in new thoughts to think. Always find a friend to go with you when hiking new trails.
5. Swimming can bring you freshness. After being in the water for any length of time can bring on a clean fresh feeling within ourselves like no other.
6. Playing golf can be the game to play for many. It allows a person time to think of so much. People of all ages enjoy taking a drive through the country, looking for where they may have hit their golf ball. Make sure to rent the floating golf cart incase you see a splash. Sorry, I couldn't resist a little joke in that last remark.
7. Bowling is a good way to spend some leisure time and can be an exciting game once you learn the what, when and where. There is a trick to knocking down all ten pins with one ball rolled. The person running the bowling alley Pro Shop can normally show you how it's done or at least steer you in the right direction.
8. Playing music is another good pass-time especially if you know how to play the instrument. Whether it is drums, a guitar, banjo, fiddle, mandolin, piano or some horn to choose or you can just listen to a stereo, music can bring a very peaceful leisure time.
9. Playing board games can keep the mind busy and in today's day, many board games can be played on a computer. These games are where one person can play against the computer. From card games to chess boards, they're a good way to keep our minds busy.
10. There is generally always some kind of sport going on for the children. From baseball to badminton and football to basketball and don't forget to mention the good all-time favorite of volleyball or soccer.

GOAL PAPER

Michael Oliver

CONGRATULATIONS,
YOU HAVE PASSED
LESSON THREE AND
HAVE COMPLETED
THE LAST FORTY-
EIGHT HOURS
LEARNING
"EXTERMINATION"

CONTINUE WITH

ALL YOU HAVE

LEARNED AND TAKE

IT WITH YOU TO

LESSON FOUR IN

LEARNING

"SAVE TIME FOR LIFE"

DSF PLAN LESSON FOUR
SAVE TIME FOR LIFE

Instructions:
Simply follow the steps in this lesson for twenty-four hour before moving on to Lesson Five. If following the steps become difficult in the exact way they are wrote, it may be best to restart your time over when you last caught yourself doing the steps wrong. Read and fill in the blanks for each step. Study this lesson as often as you please.

Examination 3:
Now is the time to examine how much time you have spent smoking. Never make up an excuse like, "That's not the right figures," because give or take a little time either way isn't going to make that much difference. Write in your answers to the best of your knowledge. With a calculator, simply add, subtract, multiply or divide as instructed.

A. How long did it take you to smoke your cigarette back in Lesson Two, Examination 2:? _____
B. Cigarettes in a pack? _____
C. Minutes smoked each pack? _____ $A \times B = C$
D. Minutes smoked each day? _____ Lesson One
Examination 1: $A \times$ Lesson Four Examination 3: $C = D$ (How many packs do you smoke a day multiplied by minutes smoked each pack).
E. Hours smoked each day? _____ $D \div 60 = E$
(Minutes smoked each day divided by 60).
F. Hours smoked each year? _____ $E \times 365 = F$
(Hours smoked each day multiplied by 365).
G. Days smoked each year? _____ $F \div 24 = G$
(Hours smoked each year divided by 24).
H. Days spent smoking? _____ $G \times$ Lesson One
Examination 1: $H = H$ (Days smoked each year multiplied by however many years you have spent smoking).
I. Solid years spent smoking? _____ $H \div 365 = I$
(Days spent smoking divided by 365).

Step 1:

Lesson Two, Examination 2, you were to keep time on two cigarettes. The time you wrote down on your Goal paper for the cigarette called, "Sitting and burning," that total time is how long you will have during your smoking time from now on as long as you wish to continue smoking. Try not to take any time less or any time more than that amount of time.

Step 2:

"The one I smoked," from Lesson Two Examination 2, however many minutes it took you to smoke your cigarette, that will be how many puffs you can take from your cigarette during your smoking time. Example, four minutes will equal four puffs from your cigarette during your smoking time. Allow your cigarette to sit in your ashtray for at least one minute between puffs. If by chance your cigarette burns out before you get all your puff, don't allow yourself to light another cigarette to make up for the lost puffs, do without. It will be best to sit and finish your smoking time even if there are no more puffs left and try not to put your cigarette out early either. Allow your cigarette time to burn out.

Step 3:

For the _____ called, "Sitting and burning," that _____ _____ is how long you will have during your smoking time from _____ _____ as long as you wish to continue smoking. Try not to take _____ _____less or any time _____ than that amount of time.

"_____ _____ __ _____," from Lesson Two Examination 2, however many minutes it took you to smoke your cigarette, that will be how many _____ you can take from your cigarette _____ your smoking _____. Example, four minutes will equal four puffs from your cigarette during your smoking time. Allow your cigarette to sit in your _____ for at least _____ _____ between puffs. If by chance your cigarette burns out before you get all your puff, _____ allow yourself to light another cigarette to make up for the _____ puffs, do without. It will be best to sit and finish your smoking time even though there are no more puffs left and try not to _____ your cigarette _____ _____ either. Allow your cigarette time to _____ _____.

DSF PLAN LESSON FOUR
SUGGESTIONS/ACTIVITIES LIST

Suggestions:

1. Sometimes, it may help to look toward the heavens and ask your God for help. The One responsible for creating believers in Him to live life, must know how to help His believers when they are in the need for help. Think about if you created a robot. If your creation needed help, who has the knowledge to give the support?

2. You may notice having more spare time since you are not smoking as much anymore. This would be a great time to do the other things you haven't had time to do. Try to find things to do that will help you use your mind more wisely without smoking. Staying busy will help keep your mind busy taking in new thoughts to think.

3. Most of the time when one person lights a cigarette, this triggers others who smoke to light up also. Keep a close watch on this situation and plan for it differently. Simply plan to not smoke when someone else is smoking. This can be fun especially if three or more smokers are in the same room. Just sit back and watch what happens when one person lights up a cigarette, how many more smokers will do the same without thinking. But, you though, have control.

4. Study all you have learned so far. Believe in yourself. Really, you do have what it takes to overpower anything in your life. Never ever settle for less than what you really want. Keep reminding yourself in every way you think a thought to think. Nobody can help you more than yourself to becoming successful.

5. Don't worry about sleepless nights. People should be more confident within themselves. It is best if they would listen to their body talk when it comes down to resting. If you can't sleep, then simply don't try to force yourself to sleep. Your body really does know how much sleep you will need to make it through your next day tomorrow and without you worrying about what you need.

6. If you feel tired and think you would like to sleep, take a book to bed with you. A book is a good way to help relax you to sleep.

Activities:

1. Hobbies can be the right activity for you. Building cars, ships, airplanes, but hobbies aren't just models. Woodworking, knitting, sewing, cooking, gardening and I would even suppose we could make a hobby out of housework. Today, computers can be a hobby and anyone can get involved pretty easily.

2. The Internet is a way to occupy your valuable spare time. There is so much information out there today and it is free to research whatever subject you would like to find out more about. Ask your nearest computer store such as "Best Buy," "Walmart," how and where you can go to get yourself up and running online?

3. Playing with your children can be a good activity for you and them. There is way too much neglect because in most families of today, both parents work to support the family income. If you have spare valuable time, try to use it wisely with your children.

4. Doing yard work is a great activity. Beside good exercise, keeping up with the growth of a beautiful yard can improve the property value if you ever decide to sell.

5. Planning a vegetable garden can be a great activity if you have good sunshine and space in your back yard. One could save a lot of money when planting their own pride of a vegetable garden.

6. Lifting weights is a good activity, but don't over do it. If you think you might want to try heavier weights, always have a friend or spotter there with you who can lift weights also.

7. Playing billiards/pool is a great activity with someone in the right location. Of course at a pool hall and try to find the ones with a smoke-free atmosphere wherever you plan to go.

8. Jogging or running on a treadmill is a great pass-time. It can be fun, along with giving a person a good workout. Depending on your age, it's not a good idea to jog on hard surfaces such as blacktop or cement. Dry grass is probably the best soft surface besides wet sand at the beach. A good running shoe built to give you cushioning while absorbing the shock from each step, is a requirement whether you have a soft surface to run on or not.

GOAL PAPER

Michael Oliver

CONGRATULATIONS,

YOU HAVE PASSED

LESSON FOUR AND

HAVE COMPLETED

THE LAST TWENTY-

FOUR HOURS

LEARNING

"SAVE TIME FOR LIFE"

CONTINUE WITH

ALL YOU HAVE

LEARNED AND TAKE

IT WITH YOU TO

LESSON FIVE IN

LEARNING

"DOING WITHOUT"

DSF Plan Lesson Five
Doing Without

Instructions:

Simply follow the steps in this lesson for seventy-two hours before moving on to Lesson Six. If following the steps become difficult in the exact way they are wrote, it may be best to restart your time over when you last caught yourself doing the steps wrong. Read and fill in the blanks to the best of your knowledge.

Examination 4:

How many hours do you sleep during the night? Whether you sleep during the day or night because of your job, how many hours do you sleep? _____ sleeping hours

A: The hours you wrote for sleeping hours, you will now call "Proved hours." _____ proved hours

B: Your own proved hours are simply the length of time, your brain knows, that you can go without smoking. And without you even ever thinking about smoking either. Never ever change your proved hours during this lesson because your brain is automatic when it comes to your own proved hours. Your brain really does know what you need and without you ever having to think about it.

Step 1:

Plan your morning ahead the night before. Plan to go consciously however many proved hours you have without smoking and do it. Don't change your proved hours in anyway. Don't add hours to your proved hours at anytime during this lesson. For example, you may figure, $7 + 7 = 14$, so now I can go 14 hours instead of my proved hours 7. Forget this and stick to your proved hours.

Simply plan your morning or night depending on your sleeping habits because of you job, plan to go your proved hours consciously in the morning time without smoking. One hour or so before your proved hours time is up, plan to go for another set of proved hours time without smoking. Continue to plan while you are awake and before your proved hours time is up, plan to go another set of proved hours without smoking.

Keep reminding yourself, you know you can go your proved hours time without smoking, because you prove it when you sleep. Say it, **"I know I can go my proved hours time without smoking, because I prove it when I sleep!"**

Step 2:
Remember where you are and why you are there. If you're at your job, you may need to tell yourself, "I came to work to work, not to smoke." Wherever you are, remember why you're there.

Step 3:
Don't buy cigarettes or any other kind of tobacco products for the rest of your life. Don't allow anyone else to buy them for you either.

Step 4:
Keep striving forward and don't turn back. Keep your mind thinking about graduation day. How good you are going to feel when you are in total control of every thought you think without smoking? What plans are you going to make for your new life ahead of you?

Step 5:
From now on and for the rest of your life, change the rules for what you do when you feel an urge to smoke. Instead of smoking, take a cup of coffee outside with you when you feel the urge to smoke. This way you are not changing the entire routine, just the smoking part of the routine. Take a break outside with your coffee, bottled water or whatever else is your cup of tea. This will give you the same satisfaction that you got from smoking a cigarette. Go outside as many times as you feel the need. Stand up if you want.

Incidence:
At times, you may experience the loss of a thought do to an unfilled habit you haven't yet fulfilled. When you try to add another thought, your mind goes blank or the old habit you don't want is all you can think of. For example, the old smoking habit you didn't fulfill and the new habit of walking to your car. When you feel stuck in the middle and have lost your train of thought, change the way you walk to your car. Take a different route that requires you to think each step out without depending on the habit like you would normally do.

DSF Plan Lesson Five
Suggestions/Activities List

Suggestions:
1. Plan before doing anything. This will help you to keep your mind full of thoughts you wish to think. It will also help you to shut out thoughts you don't wish to think. Plan everything good. Then, when you are ready to do what you've planned, try to do exactly how you had it planned.
2. Examine yourself. What were some of your reasons for starting smoking? Remember that first time and whom you were with? What are your reasons for wanting to stop? Write all your answers on your Goal Paper.
3. Get the definitions from a dictionary to help you learn what most people never seem to consider. Simple words like Cigarette, Demolish, Nervous, Nicotine, Numb, Smoking, Tobacco and of course, look up a few other words of your own. Take notes because I am sure it will shock you what you will learn. Keep thinking why you wish to Demolish Smoking Forever.
4. You may need to reach with your thoughtfulness somewhere you have never reached before on your special day. But, don't just think about it, give yourself your best of what you have for this day. If you slip, don't give up. Try your hardest to do better for your future. You have what it takes and let yourself know you have. Let yourself know you've got to do this for yourself. You've got to know exactly how it feels to be in control of your every move again in your life without smoking. You need to know how it feels to be a nonsmoker after being a smoker for all the days, months and years. Keep thinking and reminding yourself of every thought to think.
5. Continue to think why you wish to demolish smoking forever. Think of as many reasons as you possibly can to think of why you wish to demolish smoking forever. Also, try to think of reasons why you wish, never to go back to where you have been. Continue to remind yourself how good you feel and why you need to keep looking forward, to take control of your every move again in your life.

Activities:

1. Call a friend
2. Care the maintenance for your car
3. Clean your car
4. Clean your kitchen
5. Create a new look in your yard
6. Do your laundry
7. Find a new job
8. Fly a kite
9. Go Bowling/join a league
10. Go Camping/hiking
11. Go dancing with a friend
12. Go hunting
13. Go panning for gold
14. Go skating
15. Go skiing
16. Go window-shopping
17. Help a friend in need
18. Jump rope
19. Make a plan
20. Paint your house
21. Pitch horseshoes
22. Plant some fruit trees
23. Play Basketball/shoot some hoops
24. Play handball
25. Play racquetball
26. Play soccer
27. Play tennis
28. Play with your dog
29. Read a book
30. Study your Bible
31. Shoot targets
32. Watch car racing
33. Write a letter

GOAL PAPER

Michael Oliver

CONGRATULATIONS,

YOU HAVE PASSED

LESSON FIVE AND

HAVE COMPLETED

THE LAST SEVENTY-

TWO HOURS

LEARNING

"DOING WITHOUT"

CONTINUE WITH

ALL YOU HAVE

LEARNED AND TAKE

IT WITH YOU TO

LESSON SIX IN

LEARNING

"REFINED LIFE"

DSF Plan Lesson Six
Refined Life

Instructions:

Congratulations _____

You have made quite an effort in your life. You've made all the right decisions. Now, you deserve to be at this final lesson. This final lesson is for you for life. Simply follow the final steps below and you will have all the strength needed to demolish smoking forever.

Step 1:

You have made your proved hours for the past seventy-two hour and now it is time to add hours to your proved hours. Without smoking for each day that passes, you will add one hour to your proved hours. When you reach a total of twenty-four proved hours, that will be graduation day. On your calendar starting with today's date, write on this day your proved hours.

For example, if you have 7 proved hours, write the number 7 on your calendar on today's date. Tomorrow you will add 1 hour to your proved hours, writing 8 on your calendar for tomorrows date in this example. Fill in your calendar adding 1 hour to your proved hours for each day that passes until you have reached 24 proved hours on your calendar. Don't worry if you run into the next month, because this will be fine. When you are finished writing your proved hours to 24 hours, you will then know which day will be graduation day for you.

Step 2:

Don't worry about time, because you have plenty of it now. Continue to study and you will have no trouble now and forever to come. You may decide to try and conquer another unwanted routine in your life. For best results, take care of one habit at a time. Finish building your proved hours to 24 first. Then take care of all your other unwanted routines if you want after you graduate from this one.

Step 3:

Never ever think for a moment that you are the only one on this planet earth trying to stop smoking. Think of a classroom filled with students. Don't stop there with your thoughts, think of that classroom being larger than any city you could ever imagine. Think of all the graduates including yourself.

Step 4:

In your spare time, make sure you continue to study your Goal Paper notes and DSF Plan. Studying will help you remember where you've been and what you have been through to get to where you are now. Study DSF Plan anytime you please, even after you graduate.

Step 5:

At the back of this guide, there is space enough for you to write a short story of your own. Write a story on your computer first or on some sheets of binder paper to practice your writing skills. Then when you have your story perfected, transfer it over to the goal paper called "My Very Own Story" on page 47.

Start out with your name, the date you started smoking, who you were with, how much did one pack cost, why you wish to stop, the date you started DSF Plan and your completion date. Write down your memories and how DSF Plan worked out for you. Think creative

THE PRICE WE MUST PAY

Everyone must pay a price to accomplish good results. It is not easy to find such contents along with a matched price to pay for such material. But, the price was given supreme thoughtfulness before reaching the bargaining price. It's a price all DSF Plan users will have to pay. I only hope you will try and put yourself in my place of how much effort went into the creation of DSF Plan. Then you may have the understanding that the price you had to pay is only a fraction of the price I had to pay. I'll just bet it was a bargain too.

GOAL PAPER

Michael Oliver

Proven Attitude

As creator of DSF Plan, it is simple why this program worked out for me and how it should work for anyone smoking thinking of quitting. See, during the creation, I did the steps as I created them. I had no doubt in my mind that anything different from demolishing smoking forever from my life would happen.

To let you know how I did this program for myself and how it worked out for me, let me tell you, it almost worked out as planned. I was so excited about DSF Plan, that I didn't really want to spend anymore time than I had to in creating it. I couldn't wait to stop smoking after all the planning and learning so much about myself. Things I didn't even think of learning as I was planning, came out into the open. Not quite doing all the specified hours as others should, but as far as the plan itself, I stayed right with the step by steps to the end.

I planned starting DSF Plan Tuesday, February first, Nineteen ninety-four. On Monday, January thirty-first, I read Lesson One and planned on doing it the next day February first. It was easy for me to not carry my cigarettes in my pockets. But, I was very shocked when I first examined myself. It was hard for me to believe I have spent close to twenty-eight thousand dollars already on smoking cigarettes. That could have been my new car.

The evening of February first, I read Lesson Two and planned it for the next day Wednesday, February second. Most of the smoking I was doing was out on the back porch at home. So taking smoking out of my house and from my car didn't seem to be that hard, knowing I could still smoke outside somewhere else.

A few hours before bed on February second, I read Lesson Three and planned to do it the next day Thursday, February third. All the steps in this lesson I learned as I wrote them. I tried to eliminate every possible entry of how I ever got my hands on a cigarette. Step Five wasn't that hard to do, it was just different.

I read Lesson Four the evening of February third and making plans to do that lesson Friday, February forth. Again was another examination that shocked me after I found out more news about my life. Finding out I have spent close to three and some thirds solid years smoking cigarettes was a shock to me. That is like, 28,908 hours of solid smoking. I really know why I wish to stop smoking. Doing the steps make smoking seem a little harder.

Friday evening, February forth, I read Lesson Five and planned to do without smoking starting Saturday, February fifth for seventy-two hours. On February fifth, at six-thirty in the morning, I smoked three cigarettes. On February sixth, Sunday at one in the morning, again I smoked three cigarettes, one right after the other. The same day at twelve fifteen in the afternoon I smoked one cigarette. After thinking for a while I had to add one more step to Lesson Five. After changing the rules for my routine I was able to complete my seventy-two hours at twelve-thirty in the afternoon on February ninth.

After reading Lesson Six, I got my calendar and starting on day nine of February, Nineteen ninety-four, I wrote down my seven proved hours on my calendar on today's date the ninth (9). After writing an (8) in the (10) tenth day of February and so forth until I had my twenty-four proved hours wrote down on my calendar. I now know that on February 26, 1994 is going to be my graduation day. I knew it was going to take seventeen more days to complete DSF Plan. So it came to pass, Saturday, February twenty-sixth, was my last day of building my proved hours up to twenty-four hours and I have completed DSF Plan successfully.

The way I see it for my life now is, I owe it to myself to do without, for the same number of years in my life that I did smoke. This gives my mind enough time to know I am not going to be worrying about smoking until another twenty-three years have past.

In this newer version of DSF Plan, I would like to share with you while I edit the page. It has been twenty years since I completed DSF Plan. I feel great. The day I started building my proved hours up, I felt great. I couldn't believe how easy it was to let go this time. I have told many people to this day what DSF Plan has done for me. DSF Plan will be published as "Educated Smoker" and hoping some day soon will be translated worldwide.

I'VE ALREADY

DSF Plan from the beginning to the end, was created to help build self-confidence within myself. Everything worked out in a totally different aspect, from any other time, I had ever tried to quit smoking. It was fun to walk around my friends and loved ones, knowing what I knew. Knowing that they didn't even have a clue to what I was doing, because I didn't tell them. Talking to everyone was just as natural as me living any other day. I did it with my own free will, without hearing any garbage talk and cut downs. It was that much easier for me to demolish smoking forever from my life. The positive thinking that came from me really made a big difference to me, for me in helping myself. There wasn't any pressure talk from family or friends to defend against.

Then, the way DSF Plan started out and through to the end, I felt like the plan never really ever said, to stop smoking. It does say to do without, but that doesn't really seem the same as "Quit Now." The plan allowed me to choose for myself, in helping me to make all the right decisions. The lessons were so easy to follow that I didn't feel I had to quit completely all at once. Then, the way I did stop smoking, was so unexplainable at the time I did quit. It took me about one month to figure out what really happened. Why I could quit and why it seemed so easy after I did. Crazy thing was, my family didn't even sense that I quit, because I kept my same routine, but without smoking.

I am having a hard time understanding why I feel the way I do. I feel strong enough now that I will never go back to smoking. What I felt about smoking years ago is a dream to me now in my life. Feeling almost like I have never smoked a cigarette in my life is beginning to feel good. Why would I ever think about trying it out after knowing all I know? I never dreamed I would ever feel this way especially after being a non-smoker for such a short time. I love the way I feel and I am also thinking more about myself now because I can easily think clearer. I have wondered strangely about something years ago and today I am there. Back then, I knew what was right and still I smoked knowing the truth. Today I'm past that stage knowing the truth and I don't smoke. It is such a wonderful feeling to be able to live in the truth, knowing what is right.

After two weeks of using DSF Plan, my fellow workers finally found out that I didn't smoke anymore. It was kind of funny, at the right given time, everyone will know. That will be when everyone shares the joy of a new born together.

I went to a business meeting away from home. A few weeks earlier, the rooms were ordered. Yes, they ordered me a smoking room as they always had in the past. While confirming the room, I had already started DSF Plan and wasn't to share it with anyone. At the time, I figured, I would re-order at the hotel on that very day.

Naturally the day came to leave to the meeting. When we arrived at the hotel and were checking in, I asked if there were any non-smoking rooms available? Naturally there were none available. It was kind of funny, because Clark Watanabe, the field rep I rode with to the meeting for the last few hours said, "What? Did you quit?" I didn't say anything hoping nothing else would be said. That evening at a company gathering, the big boys had heard I quit smoking. This was when I didn't mind answering their questions with the truth. It was the greatest feeling I ever had, waiting for the right given time, to share the happiness together with my friends and co-workers. Funny thing is, they all seemed to believe me at this right given time. There was no pressure, nothing to prove at this right given time to anyone. Which only goes the show, there is a difference between the sayings, "I'm going to do it" and "I've already."

June 1, 1994 I had sent DSF Plan to the Copyright Office to register. The greatest thing in my life was to quit smoking and I did it by using DSF Plan. I love to talk and share with those who like to listen. Some of the people I have told, smoke, some have quit, some have never smoked and others have asked if they could try using DSF Plan. People can often help others best by sharing their own experiences.

Today, Christmas Day, 2013, I am re-editing and bringing this book up-to-date preparing to register once again with the Copyright Office for this new title; "Educated Smoker"

THE END

My Very Own Story

Michael Oliver

Michael Oliver

Michael Oliver

_____

_____

_____

_____

_____

_____

_____

_____

_____

_____

_____

_____

_____

_____

_____

_____

_____

_____

_____

_____

_____

_____

_____

_____

_____

_____

_____

_____

_____

Michael Oliver

Michael Oliver

Michael Oliver